# Worshipping Through John

## A Devotional for Praise Teams

Aaron Reimer

ISBN: 0993806902
ISBN-13: 978-0993806902 (Broken Arise Books)

# INTRODUCTION

Most praise teams are passionate about seeing their congregation grow in their worship and closeness with God. A key element in helping that to happen is growing and developing themselves, both spiritually and technically. As a worship pastor, and a person passionate about seeing people develop their gifts to the fullest as they serve God, I've found that one of the greatest ways to accomplish this is to being in scripture together, talking about shared ministry, and praying with each other. Also, making music, but this is less about that than the rest of it.

Worshipping Through John is an opportunity is to have the whole praise team work through the book of John together and process some of the questions that are important in developing a vision of personal and corporate worship. The following is how I'd suggest it be used, but every team is unique and leaders should freely adapt the devotional process for them:

Plan 10-15 minutes for devotion time:

1. Have a short time of sharing about life
2. Have someone read the scripture out loud
3. Read the focus verse
4. Read the devotion
5. Discuss the questions
6. Pray

Alternate use:

1. Provide each member of the worship team with a copy of the devotional
2. Challenge each person to read and pray through the relevant devotion on their own time, consider the questions, and come to practice with thoughts.
3. Have a five minute discussion and prayer time at the beginning of practice.

Note on capitalization: Pronouns referring to God the Father, Son, or Holy Spirit are not capitalized in keeping with the style of the NIV translation.

## Witnesses To The Light

Read: John 1:1-18

Focus: John 1:6-8

*There was a man sent from God whose name was John. He came as a witness to testify concerning the light, so that through him all might believe. He himself was not the light; he came only as a witness to the light.*

John the Baptist was described first and foremost as a man sent from God. In the Greek, the description is more than a mission, though, it's the core of who he was. He was a *sent-from-God-man*! Bearing witness to the light was more than something he did; it was central to his identity. That sent-from-God identity isn't a unique thing to those prophets with a "special" mission. Jesus commissioned his disciples to go and tell the world about him; all that he had taught, and all they had seen him do. They went with joy and amazement, made bold by all that had been shown to them.

We are sent people, called to be a witness to the light. We follow in the footsteps of John the Baptist, telling the world about the light of Christ. For worship leaders particularly, Sunday morning is a special time of witness. We are encouraging and assisting our church family to testify to who God is and what he's done. We, as a congregation, bear witness to how amazing our living savior is, for each other and for the seekers and unchurched people who join us on a Sunday morning! In our worship, we shine light in the spiritual realm as the angels rejoice and the demons tremble. We are sent-from-God to do it. He has trusted us with that. How humbling. How magnificent. May it become the very core of who we are.

1. What about our worship bears witness to the light?
2. Is there anything that hinders that witness or could give it a greater impact?

**Prepare Ye The Way**

Read: John 1:19-28

Focus: John 1:23

*John replied in the words of Isaiah the prophet, "I am the voice of one calling in the wilderness, 'Make straight the way for the Lord.'"*

John the Baptist knew who he was. People flocked to him to hear him speak and were moved by his message. They were drawn to him by reports of both his strange appearance and behavior, and the passion with which he preached. Sometimes the things that he was doing seemed a bit odd or out of place, but he had a mission. He had an answer for the people who asked him what he was all about. He had a definite purpose and was pursuing it wholeheartedly. When he had to define it, he referred back to Scripture, saying that he was a person called to make straight the way for the Lord.

That meant that his mission was preparing people's hearts to receive the message of Christ. That is a wonderful job description for a worship team. We are called to make a straight way for the Lord. Part of our mission is helping people shift their focus from where they've been to where they are. We are helping people move past the baggage that's weighing on them, and we're waging a spiritual battle to make the enemy who would distract them unwelcome. This isn't just about getting people ready for a sermon, but about clearing the way for a connection with God. If people are inwardly focused and closed off from God, everything is entertainment at best. When people open themselves to God's voice, he can speak from anything, be it scripture, song, visual, or message.

1. What are some things that hinder people from focusing on God?
2. What can we as a worship team do to "make straight the way for the Lord?"

## The Voice of Experience

Read: John 1:29-34

Focus: John 1:34

*"I have seen and I testify that this is God's Chosen One."*

For John the Baptist, seeing Jesus enter the water meant the culmination of his life's work. More than that, though, the Spirit of God confirmed to him that he was having a true encounter with God's promised messiah. What a relief and abundance of joy he must have felt to know that the one he had waited for was truly there! More than just believing in the possibility, he now had firsthand knowledge of the reality. He would never be the same. An encounter with God changes people. Sometimes there's a physical sign of the experience, like Moses. Other times people are healed of a disability or sickness – blindness, lameness, even leprosy. Most often, the change comes inside their spirits, evidenced by changed lives. The most common response to these changes is the joyful proclamation of God's wonderful works.

As a worship team, each Sunday we are privileged to help people give voice to the awesomeness of God. We sing about the things he's done for us, the qualities that make him worthy of praise, and our continually renewed commitment to him. The heart of worship is that testimony. When the congregation stands up to sing, we proclaim Jesus. When we are at our most passionate, it's usually because those words and that music connect us with an experience of God's presence in our lives; when we can honestly and truly say that *we have seen.* In our worship, we proclaim to each other, and the world, that we have seen and testify that Jesus is God's Chosen One.

1. What is one area or event in your life where you have seen the work of God's Chosen One?
2. How have we seen God moving at our church?

**More Than Facts**

Read: John 1:35-51

Focus: John 1:38-39

*Jesus saw them following and asked, "What do you want?"*
*They said, "Rabbi . . . where are you staying?"*
*"Come," he replied, "and you will see."*
*So they went and saw where he was staying, and they spent that day with him.*

It was a simple question of geography: "Where are you staying?" John's disciples were asking for a fact that they could add to their knowledge. Jesus didn't respond with a fact, though, he responded with an invitation. He didn't give them the answer they wanted. Instead, he gave the one they needed. They didn't need information, they needed him. When they responded to his invitation and followed him, their desire changed from information to formation. They didn't just take in the location and return to tell the people who sent them. They stopped and stayed in his presence.

As worship leaders, we often face the temptation of a quick stop with Jesus. We do a five-minute devotional and move on to practice. We get all the scripture we need in order to plan a transition or introduce songs and bring it to the congregation. We get what they've asked for and bring it to them. When we really spend time with Jesus, though, we focus our sense of relationship and intensify our personal worship. We go back with more than they asked for. When our worship leading comes from a place inside, from our closeness with Christ, there's an authenticity that makes people long for the same. We bring them what they need.

1. When was the last time you "spent the day" with Jesus?
2. Do you think a day spent with Jesus can involve running around and all sorts of excitement, or should it be a day of peace and retreat?

## More Than Music

Read: John 2:1-11

Focus: John 2:8

*Then he told them, "Now draw some out and take it to the master of the banquet."*

Music is important to musicians. There's something in it that resonates. When things are tight, and everyone is playing and singing perfectly together, and the song is brilliantly crafted, it can give way to shivers and tears. That makes sense to us – we're wired that way. All the same, though, the resonance and emotion that great music brings is of this world. The feeling can come from well crafted secular music just as easily as sacred. It has the power to move emotionally for a time, but the feeling fades. No matter how great the emotion or technicality of the music, it doesn't compare to the power of an experience of the Spirit of God through the conduit of a song.

The simple fact is that what we draw out and bring to the congregation is water. We can, of ourselves, draw sludge water, or river water, or filtered water, or even fancy carbonated mineral water, but at the heart of it, it's just water. That's okay. It's all we're called to do. It takes an act of God to make it more than a song. Something amazing happens when we open up with sincere worship and allow God to make a home in the music. It's only God who can take the words and music we bring and turn it into a miraculous encounter with him. He changes what we can produce and makes it worthy. He takes our water and makes it wine.

1. Can you think of a time when a song connected you to God in a supernatural way?
2. Does it matter what we sing or how we sound if God is capable of turning any offering into meaningful worship?

**A Slow Slide**

Read: John 2:12-25

Focus: John 2:16-17

*... He said, "Get these out of here! Stop turning my Father's house into a market!" His disciples remembered that it is written: "Zeal for your house will consume me."*

When Jesus came to the temple, the highest place of worship in the Jewish faith, he was enraged. It hadn't happened overnight. There wasn't one day that the people of God were worshipping passionately in Spirit and Truth, and the next buying "special" sacrifices and "official" offering money at a wicked exchange. It was a slow change. The meaning was lost in the method. Perhaps the first animal sellers truly desired to give people the means to make the most pleasing sacrifices to God that they could. Perhaps the first money changers wanted to serve the people by conveniently changing Roman currency to a form acceptable to the priests. They were certainly authorised by the religious leadership as a welcome ministry.

What happened? Somehow the ministries in the temple court had gone from an act of service to callous greed that infuriated the Son of God. In this, scripture provides us with a frightening object lesson in what church can become. Are we in danger of that in our own congregations? How can we tell? One of the key steps toward the slide seen in the temple is the loss of zeal for God's house. When church becomes ordinary and formulaic; when worship becomes stagnant; when the awe of the Lord fades and expectancy diminishes, consumerism sets in. Church becomes about us, and what we can get out of it. God's house slowly becomes our house because, inevitably, the more the focus rests on us, the less zeal we have for the presence of God.

1. How do you think Jesus would feel in our services?
2. What excites you about coming to church?

## They Might Not Get It

Read: John 3:1-15

Focus: John 3:11

*Very truly I tell you, we speak of what we know, and we testify to what we have seen, but still you people do not accept our testimony.*

Jesus was like no other teacher they'd seen. His disciples had been with him only a short time, but miracles, signs, and wonders had been flowing out of his ministry, and they were bold about telling the people they encountered. They were seeing Heaven poured out on Earth, and it was hard to explain to anyone who wasn't experiencing it. Even for some people that had dedicated their lives to serving God, it felt odd, uncomfortable, maybe dangerous. It didn't fit their paradigm of who and what God was. It didn't click.

When we stand up on Sunday morning, our worship is (or should be) an outpouring of our experience. Our connection with God brings passion and excitement. It gives us a reason to sing, and personal truth behind lyrical offerings. It can be disconcerting when we look out into the congregation and there are people who aren't joining in. It could be one guy at the back with a sour look on his face and his hands in his pockets or half the congregation looking bored or uncomfortable. It could be that there are group dynamics involved, or spiritual oppression. Maybe we're just bringing new songs into a congregation that likes the familiar. Maybe we're challenging people to go deeper than they want to go. Sometimes seeing that apathy or resistance can be disheartening, but we need to remember that it's nothing new to those who would be witnesses for God's kingdom come.

1. How do you feel when you look out and the worship doesn't seem to be connecting with people?
2. What can we do to keep our personal worship focused when things feel flat?

**Pulled In Every Direction**

Read: John 3:16-21

Focus: John 3:17

*For God did not send his Son into the world to condemn the world, but to save the world through him.*

It's possible that there's never been a person both more praised and more reviled than Jesus Christ. The way people whose lives he entered into responded to him had less to do with what he actually said or did, and more to do with what *they* were expecting; how entrenched they were in their ideology, their preferences and their spheres of power. Jesus entered the world at a point of turmoil and came under attack from the Right and the Left. There are many times in his ministry where he couldn't have been blamed if he'd thrown up his hands and said "I'm done with this. It's not worth it."

In the modern church, there have been few areas that have matched congregational worship in terms of entrenchment, expectation or, especially, preference. When we get up to play, it will be simultaneously too loud and too quiet, too old and too new, and have too much and too little piano (or guitar, or whatever) for some people in the congregation. Some of them will be vocal about it. Like Jesus, it may help to remember two things: It's ultimately God who has given us a mission and we are serving, and it's not about us. That doesn't mean that serving out our mission means bowing to whichever voice is loudest at the moment, but it does mean having grace, love and compassion for people who disagree with us.

1. How do you feel when you're in the context of a practice and the leader (or another team member) asks you to do something different than what you're doing?
2. Why do you think people react so strongly when their worship preferences aren't prioritized?

**Listening For The Voice**

Read: John 3:22-36

Focus: John 3:29

*The friend who attends the bridegroom waits and listens for him, and is full of joy when he hears the bridegroom's voice.*

The image in this brief parable is one of purpose, expectation, and longing. The friend of the bridegroom was to witness the completion of the wedding ritual. He wasn't the focus of the ceremony, but he had an important place as the one who would announce to the people that the wedding was final. He was tense and eager, waiting for his moment to be part of something so special. He knew it was coming, and when it did - joy. This was how John the Baptist saw his role in the union of the Messiah with the people of God.

As worship team members, how do we react to the voice of God? Do we anticipate it with excitement, or are we surprised and distrustful if ever we hear it? Surely it can be difficult to lead when we don't. As we prepare to announce the bridegroom, do we listen for his voice? Devotions and prayer, scripture reading, personal worship: these are all things that we can engage in with hopeful purpose, or blow through to get at the immediate technical concerns of worship leading, individually or as a team. Our first desire should be his voice, not ours. The voice of God should fill us with a joy that is infectious to the people we're called to lead. This is the purpose that God has called us to: to listen for the voice of the bridegroom, and to announce it with great joy!

1. Can you describe a time that you feel you heard God's voice?
2. Before closing in prayer, spend at least 2 minutes in silence with God (adjust at the discretion of the worship team leader).

**In The Spirit and Truth**

Read: John 4:1-26, 39-42

Focus: John 4:23

*"Yet a time is coming and has now come when the true worshipers will worship the Father in the Spirit and in truth, for they are the kind of worshipers the Father seeks."*

Many, many years before Jesus, Jacob wrestled with God and was named Israel. He reconciled with his estranged brother, and went away blessed. He bought land in Canaan and dug a well. In today's passage, Jesus sat at that well with a Samaritan woman. The Samaritans were despised by the Jews, because in the intervening years, they had separated from the nation of Israel - intermarrying with the Assyrians. They were no longer a people set apart for God. They were impure and shunned. The Samaritans knew their history, though; they remembered the God of Jacob and worshiped him in their own way, but this certainly wasn't good enough for the Jews. They knew the "right way" and "right place" to worship. They wouldn't speak to Samaritans for fear of corruption, and drinking from their cup would make them ceremonially unclean.

Jesus didn't care. He broke the pattern. He said that God was much less concerned with where or how you worship than with the heart of worship offered to him. We've all got history in our worship. We all have patterns that have been significant to us and helped us connect with God. That's okay. There is a danger, though, that we can get caught up in the form of our music and forget to worship. Form can be good. It can be useful and inspiring, but we need to remember the function is the worthier part.

1. What does it mean to you to worship in Spirit and in truth?
2. Have you ever been blessed when you worshipped in a way that wasn't your comfortable norm?

## On The Shoulders of Giants

Read: John 4:27-38

Focus: John 4:38

*"I sent you to reap what you have not worked for. Others have done the hard work, and you have reaped the benefits of their labor."*

An old adage attributed to the 12th century philosopher Bernard of Chantres says that modern people are like dwarves standing on the shoulders of giants. It's a privilege that we often overlook. We like to feel self-sufficient: to do things our own way and bask in the credit when it's done. Jesus calls his disciples to humility, though. He asks us to recognise that we are part of a much larger story. Most of the great work we do for his kingdom is done on the backs of those who have come before. At the same time, we can also recognise that sometimes what he calls his disciples to is work that is going to prepare the field for someone else's harvest, and that's good, too.

We are blessed in the modern church with gifted worship leaders who have been inspired to write tremendous songs that speak to our hearts and speak our hearts to God. They seem like giants to us, inspiring us and using their music to lift our own corporate and personal worship to levels beyond where we could attain on our own. If they seem like they see more, though, it's because they're also standing on the shoulders of giants. Each generation is inspired by those that have come before. The key thing that this philosophy points us toward is to know and understand the greatness of what has come before, not throwing it out, but at the same time not being bound to it; to integrate it and let it help us grow, becoming part of a much greater story.

1. Who inspires you in your worship and why?
2. What is one thing you've learned about worship that you'd pass on to the next generation?

**The Promised Presence**

Read: John 4:43-54

Focus: John 4:50

*. . . The man took Jesus at his word and departed . . . he and his whole household believed.*

The passage today is the story of a loving and desperate father. He'd walked about 42 kilometers (20 miles) to seek out this man who he'd heard had been doing miracles. There was no guarantee that Jesus still would even be there in Cana when he arrived, but this was his last chance. A miracle from Jesus was the last hope that he was holding in his heart. Jesus' response must have shocked him completely. Here he was pleading for the life of his son, and Jesus was complaining that people wouldn't believe in him unless they kept seeing these amazing signs. The father persevered, though, and Jesus promised healing. He didn't go with him, but gave him an opportunity to believe.

As we enter into worship each week, we often call for the presence of God in our services – for his Spirit to come fill the room – and then watch eagerly to see if he does. We look for feelings to get swept up, and a sense of power in worship that we might not otherwise see. When things don't go quite right, or worship feels stale or flat, we might question where God was, or why he didn't show up. The fact is, though, Jesus has promised that where two or three are gathered in his name, he's there (Matt. 18:20). There is no question about his presence. It's there. He promised. Whether we see signs and wonders or not, we can know it's true.

1. Why can it sometimes be so hard to take God at his word?
2. How does our worship change if we assume the presence of God instead of waiting on it?

**The Water Is Warm**

Read: John 5:1-15

Focus: John 5:7

*"Sir," the invalid replied, "I have no one to help me into the pool when the water is stirred. While I am trying to get in, someone else goes down ahead of me."*

The pool of Bethseda was a place in Jerusalem where the infirm awaited miraculous healing. Tradition tells us that from time to time, an angel would stir the waters of the pool. Upon seeing this sign, the first into the water would be healed of their malady. It was a place for desperate people waiting on God. It also must have seemed incredibly unfair. Those with the smallest problem were the most likely to be first to the water. Some people with major issues were blessed to have friends there to wait with them and rush them to the pool, but for this invalid, there was no chance of him making it in first, even if he waited right beside the pool, away from the shaded areas in the heat of the day.

For some people, worship comes naturally in song. They barely need a note and they are right there, singing their hearts out to God. Some need some time to move into a place of worship. For others, there's just no way they can get there on their own. For many of them, it's not that they don't want to. They may see people moved in worship, and wish that they could have that for themselves, but there are barriers that stop them from getting there. As a worship team, it can be frustrating to look out and see people disengaged, hands in pockets, mouths closed. We'll ignore them or look past them to the people who seem to "get it." As worship leaders, though, we are the able bodied. It's our job to help them get to the pool.

1. What hinders people from being able to worship freely?
2. What helps to move you to a place of worship when you're having trouble getting there?

## A Broader Vocabulary

Read: John 5:16-30

Focus: John 5:19

*Jesus gave them this answer: "Very truly I tell you, the Son can do nothing by himself; he can do only what he sees his Father doing, because whatever the Father does the Son also does.*

"He's copying me," is one of the complaints most often heard by anyone dealing with multiple children. We can tell kids that imitation is the sincerest form of flattery, but that falls flat. They don't want to be flattered; they want to be unique. On the other hand, Christianity, at its heart, is about imitation. Jesus set an example, and called his followers to carry on in it. Paul told the church in Corinth to imitate him as he imitated Christ. Without the example set by the Son of God, those who desire to live in relationship with God have an even greater struggle trying to figure out what a life of wholehearted devotion to him should look like.

For most people, following God doesn't come naturally. It's something we learn to do through instruction, study, and watching those who have come before us. For the vast majority of people coming to church, worship is the same way. It's almost like a language to be learned. We gain vocabulary in the way we talk about God, the songs we sing, how we use our bodies and actions, and ultimately how we orient our lives towards him. One of the key functions of a worship team is to be that example for people to look at. Even without being explicitly taught, like children, we gain vocabulary from the people that lead us. Our congregations will tend to follow, and communicate in the vocabulary we show them.

1. What can we do to increase our worship vocabulary?
2. Who is one person that you learned about worship from, and one thing you learned from them?

**Spotlight**

Read: John 5:31-47

Focus: John 5:35

*John was a lamp that burned and gave light, and you chose for a time to enjoy his light.*

Since the 1990s, there has been a continually-growing trend in North America towards the Superstar Worship Leader. Off the tops of our heads, most of us can name at least a handful of worship leaders who have written half of the worship songs we sing, release piles of worship albums and have worship concerts that draw thousands of people. On the smaller church level, we've tended to follow that trend, often hiring talented, charismatic individuals to make our music more excellent and our services more exciting. There's nothing wrong with a church wanting to give God the most musically-pleasing worship they can, but a danger in our "idol" driven society is that the focus can fall on the worshipper rather than rising to the worshipped.

John the Baptist was a wild guy with a powerful message and an attention getting lifestyle. There was nothing wrong with that; that's what God called him to do. People flocked to him to hear him speak. From what Jesus is saying, though, it seems that people were coming to him to see *him*, and dismissing the one whom he preached. It can be hard for people used to worshipping what they see to transition across the worship barrier from the light of the leader to the light of the Son. Some people will always function on that level, but we need to do our best to facilitate the transition – giving them their worship voice rather than just singing along with us.

1. Why do you think we put so much focus on the worship leader?
2. How do we deal with the tension of leading people towards God and getting out of their way so they can see him?

**Famine That Brings Abundance**

Read: John 6:1-15

Focus: John 6:7

*Philip answered him, "It would take more than half a year's wages to buy enough bread for each one to have a bite!"*

The disciples must have felt like they had dropped the ball. Or Jesus had dropped the ball. *Someone* had dropped the ball. Somehow, Jesus' speaking time had run well into the time that more than 5000 people should have been eating, and there was no food for them. In fact, a rough estimate of the cost of an emergency lunch was more than a year's wages; not out of the realm of possibility for a well-funded mega-church, but well into the impossible for an itinerate rabbi and his band of followers. In one of the most well-known miracles of his ministry, Jesus takes an offering of a few loaves and fish, and leaves the crowd fed with abundance.

How is it possible that one little boy was the only one with the foresight to bring a meal? Could it be that he was the only one who was willing to offer what seemed like a uselessly small amount to Jesus? The disciples must have felt so inadequate when Jesus put the problem to them. The young boy must have felt completely inadequate handing over his small lunch. With Jesus, though, that inadequacy became a bounty. Out of the little the boy had, he held nothing back. That was the key. In our worship, there will be many times of feeling inadequate to the task, lacking ability, equipment, or preparation, but when we give to God all that we do have--not hedging based on what *we* think our offering is worth--he can multiply it more than we can imagine.

1. Have you ever experienced a situation when God made a worship time that logically should have been poor into something special?
2. Given God's ability to multiply an offering, does it matter if we put everything into the worship music we can?

## On A Boat

Read: John 6:16-24

Focus: John 6:21

*Then they were willing to take him into the boat, and immediately the boat reached the shore where they were heading.*

Jesus' disciples had just had a very long day. Anyone in the food service industry can attest to the amount of work involved in serving a large table or group function, and the disciples had just served and bussed meals for eight to ten thousand people. Jesus had withdrawn to avoid crowds that wanted to force him into their "messiah mold" and the disciples had to go on ahead. It should have been an easy jaunt for experienced fishermen – a quick sail across the lake – but they may have misjudged the timing and the weather, because they were soon rowing against the waves in the dark.

We can imagine that the disciples felt pretty confident that they could succeed despite the struggle. They made it almost all the way to the opposite side on their own, and then along came Jesus. One thing that anyone who has ever been to camp knows is how hard it is to get a person into a boat from the water, particularly when the water is rough. It would have seemed like a big risk to switch from a "get where we're going in one piece" mentality to letting Jesus in. The moment they did, though, they saw their mission accomplished. In worship, we can be the same way: dependent on our own talents and skills, particularly when the waves start rising. We get so focused on keeping the boat steady that we forget that the important thing is that Jesus be in it.

1. Do you ever become so focused on the technical aspects of the music that the spiritual aspects of worship fade?
2. How can we make God a part of our preparation for leading worship?

**Chasing "Worship"**

Read: John 6:25-59

Focus: John 6:26

*Jesus answered, "Very truly I tell you, you are looking for me, not because you saw the signs I performed but because you ate the loaves and had your fill.*

Sometimes you get the impression that Jesus might have been a bit tired of people clamouring for miracles. He fed a crowd of 5000 men, along with women and children. It must have been an awesome experience for them. Then, one minute he'd been teaching clearly about who he was in relation to the Father, as well as all their messianic hopes and dreams, and then the next he'd disappeared. The people went searching for him and found him teaching in a synagogue on the other side of the lake. Rather than being gratified that they'd followed him, he challenged their reason for doing it: they weren't coming to him for who he was; they were chasing an experience.

It's human nature, and it happens now just as much then as it did then. Churches are full of people that come, not because they are seeking God, but because they are seeking the experience of God. In a church where God has done awesome things – people have been healed, or lives have been touched, or the worship experience is incredible and emotional – people come back week after week for more. Many churches have grown by having a service of incredible "quality": exciting music, engaging teaching, and dramatic lighting. Is it pleasing to God to have churches grow this way? Are people really there worshipping God for who he is, or are they chasing a worship high? Are *we*?

1. Can you think of one incredible time of worship you've had?
2. How do you react to a time of worship when you don't feel like you've "experienced God"?

## Hard Truths

Read: John 6:60-71

Focus: John 6:60, 66

*On hearing it, many of his disciples said, "This is a hard teaching. Who can accept it?". . . From this time many of his disciples turned back and no longer followed him.*

Jesus made some pretty radical claims about himself, sometimes in front of people who had known him his entire life. His followers had been amazed at what he could do, and intrigued by what he said. Most of them were ready to accept him as a prophet, but he took it further than that: He identified himself as the Son of God, holding himself out as the provider of eternal life. Many of the people around him were unable to take the step of faith, despite all they had seen. It went against all that they believed that they knew.

There should come a time in every believer's life that the teaching of Jesus Christ becomes uncomfortable. In fact, it will probably happen many times. Our Christian lives will be defined by whether we accept what Christ says and adjust our lives to follow, or adjust our beliefs about Christ to accommodate our lifestyle and culture. If we are to be the leaders of our church we have to be Christ followers and proclaim his truth. We need to let truth be truth whether it's convenient or not, whether it's popular or not, and whether or not we lose people over it. The words we choose to offer the congregation for worship, be they hymns or modern praise songs, set the tone for truth in our churches. It's important to choose to sing the hard truths.

1. Has there ever been anything about Christianity that's hard for you to accept?
2. Should there be a line of "acceptable faith and belief" for those helping to lead worship?

**Gut Check**

Read: John 7:1-24

Focus: John 7:18

*Whoever speaks on their own does so to gain personal glory, but he who seeks the glory of the one who sent him is a man of truth; there is nothing false about him.*

When Jesus stepped up to teach at the festival, it must have been an odd sight. At an occasion like that, the best of the rabbis would have been called on; the PhDs of their time. The best and the brightest came up through the ranks of Torah, Talmud and Midrash students, hoping for a chance at the big stage. Among them, a carpenter with no higher religious education steps up and blows them away. It was a contrast, not just in style or substance, but in the core of being. Jesus challenged them on something fundamental: being a rabbi for most of them was more about honour of station than service to God.

Anyone who serves in a position of leadership needs to be doing a continual gut-check. Are we serving because we have a call from God and we *must*, or are we serving because we like the way people look at us when we play, or compliment us afterwards? It can be an uncomfortable question to contemplate. For the vast majority of us, if we're honest, it's at least a little bit of both. There are things in most of us that crave recognition and enjoy the spotlight. James tells us that the spotlight comes at a price, though: a harsher judgment by those who see us calling ourselves representatives of God. We need to keep our focus on him in all humility, so that we can see clearly the work he calls us to.

1. Why did you become involved with worship ministry?
2. What are some dangers in having a "self-focus" in leading worship?

**Overflow**

Read: John 7:25-52

Focus: John 7:37-38

*On the last and greatest day of the festival, Jesus stood and said in a loud voice, "Let anyone who is thirsty come to me and drink. Whoever believes in me, as Scripture has said, rivers of living water will flow from within them."*

The buzz around Jesus had been building. His teaching was drawing crowds, and rumors were flying. Some people were hailing him as the Messiah; others wanted to kill him. Everyone was fascinated with him. He had something that they'd never seen before. On that last day of the festival, he made a bold declaration: he was the source of satisfaction for the thirsty. The expected result of drinking the living water would be that the living water would be in them, but he took it a step farther... the living water would flow out of them too! They would become a source for those whose lives they touched.

So much of the time, we come to church to "be filled". We, the thirsty, come to drink. We encourage others to come to the fountain and be filled as well. That's good. Jesus calls us to do that. But the living water is supposed to flow from us as well. We should be serving out of an overflow. Our praise needs to be coming out of us because there's too much to hold in: it's alive inside of us, and it wants to flow out to the world. Jesus is the source of the living water, but our overflow is the evidence of it to the world. It should change us. We don't come to be served, but to serve. We praise not because it's what we want to do but because we can't not.

1. What does a person who is overflowing with living water look like?
2. Can you think of a time that you were overflowing to the point that you couldn't help but praise God?

## Letting Go

Read: John 8:1-11

Focus: John 8:9

*At this, those who heard began to go away one at a time, the older ones first, until only Jesus was left, with the woman still standing there.*

People come to Jesus with their own history and the way they think things ought to be done. Sometimes that's based on their training or life experience. Sometimes that's based on a personal agenda. Often it's based on their view of who God is. This was very true of the Pharisees and teachers of the law. They dragged a woman caught in adultery to Jesus because they believed that they knew what ought to be done and they wanted to make Jesus do it. Jesus, as he is apt to do, somehow turned it on its head.

In clashes of church culture, everyone enters in with strongly held beliefs. Most often, the divide falls between old and new: the way things have been done, and the way the next generation thinks they ought to be done. Bitter battles over the culture of worship have divided many churches. In this passage, we see Jesus communicating his side to the accusers. It's interesting to note that the older ones left first. Maybe it was because they had the wisdom to accept Jesus' point. More likely it's because the younger ones tend to be more tenacious and hot-headed on most issues. Many evangelical churches are losing the older generation because the younger generation holds more strongly to the way they think it should be. Jesus is not honored by either attitude. Maybe, if we can shift our hearts to praising God rather than praising the worship of God, both the old and the young can let go of their entrenchment.

1. Have you ever been in a conflict about "the way worship should be"?
2. In your opinion, what are some keys to avoiding "worship wars"?

**Awesome God**

Read: John 8:12-30

Focus: John 8:23

*But he continued, "You are from below; I am from above. You are of this world; I am not of this world.*

Sometimes it's hard to get our heads around Jesus. As we study his life and seek to emulate him, as we draw close to him, we become incredibly aware of how human he was. He was like us. He knows our struggles. We can know him and relate to him. In the midst of that, it can be difficult to remember that, at the same time he's fully human, he's fully divine. He's immanent (close and knowable), but also transcendent (extending beyond the bounds of experience and comprehension). It's part of what makes him so compelling: there is a depth to Jesus that we'll never be able to fully comprehend.

Often, we sing our worship songs as if we are singing to a friend or a lover or a king. We use the human metaphors we have been taught to help us understand him and relate on a human level. We lose the majesty and otherness of God. The power of theology in music is cyclical: the way we think about God forms the lyrics we choose or write, and the lyrics we sing, in turn, form our thoughts about God. They form our congregation's thoughts about God. It can become easy, when we relate to God like he's "like us, but better," for him to become progressively smaller in our eyes. God is more than redeemer and friend... he is the majestic author of **everything**. The entire universe was made at his command from nothing. Fear and awe of God is the beginning of wisdom. When we are presenting songs, we need to remember his awesomeness along with his loving closeness.

1. What puts you in awe of God?
2. What are some songs that speak to you about God's amazing otherness?

**Not To Us**

Read: John 8:31-59

Focus: John 8:50

*[Jesus said,] I am not seeking glory for myself; but there is one who seeks it, and he is the judge.*

Jesus has a unique relationship with his followers. One of the core differences is that he is both the one we worship and our model for ministry. During his time on earth, he didn't try to glorify himself. He didn't look for fame, or accolades or the approval of his friends and family. While he likely didn't refuse compliments on a good sermon, that wasn't the reason he stood up. Jesus' entire ministry was centred on bringing glory to God the Father in heaven through revealing him on Earth. Scripture tells us that after his ministry was complete, he ascended to heaven to receive the glory due to him as God the Son.

It's odd to think that God seeks glory, but the Bible tells us he does. Knowing that, our job as God's people is simple: to give it to him. As worship leaders, we assist our people in one facet of that, which is to glorify him in song. That means that everything we do should point people to God. We need to examine our motivations and see that our focus is not on us but on him. Throughout our worship service and afterwards, people should be thinking about God. They should walk out thinking about how awesome he is and how amazing the things he does are. We help give them a voice to do that. As we take the platform, we have to remember that we are there to help people give God the glory he desires. What an incredible mission!

1. How do we glorify God on Sunday morning?
2. Have you ever been present in a worship service when your attention wasn't on God? Please share.

**Where's Jesus?**

Read: John 9:1-12

Focus: John 9:12

*"Where is this man?" they asked him. "I don't know," he said.*

Jesus had just worked an incredible miracle. He didn't just heal sight that had been taken away, but gave the blind man something that he had never had before. With spit and mud, Jesus took something from himself, blended it with the raw material that God had made the first people from, and used it to give this man something that he was born without. In the same way, his blood, spilled on the earth beneath the cross, gives us a righteousness and spiritual vision we were born without: an even greater miracle!

The blind man had a life-changing encounter with Jesus Christ. When asked about it, he could relate the details, and was glad to testify to them. When his questioners inquired as to the present location of Jesus, though, he was at a loss. Our churches are full of people like this. Maybe at some point in their lives, they met Jesus. They prayed a prayer and accepted his grace for their sin, but never made the transition to having Christ as the ever present Lord of their lives. Some churches are even like that: possessing the right words, but the Spirit of God conspicuously absent from their midst. It's a tough question: Do you know where Jesus is? Is he someone you encountered on the road, or an ever-present part of your life? On Sunday mornings, our people come to us asking where Jesus is and we need to be able to point the way.

1. Have you even had a season of your life (or are you in one now) when you weren't sure where God was?
2. How do we respond when the Spirit of God doesn't seem present in our church?

**Amazing Grace**

Read: John 9:13-34

Focus: John 9:25

*He replied, "Whether he is a sinner or not, I don't know. One thing I do know. I was blind but now I see!"*

Testifying to a personal encounter with God can be difficult when we're dealing with a world that wants to explain him away. The man who had been blind had never seen Jesus, but he knew who had given him sight. Questioned by people who were heavily invested in having their religious views be right, he was encouraged at great social penalty to deny the one who had just given him sight. In response, he offered the blunt truth: he didn't understand all of the dynamics of what had happened, but he couldn't fail to witness to the work of Christ in his life.

In his famous hymn, "Amazing Grace," John Newton references this passage, declaring "I once was lost, but now am found; was blind, but now I see." For some Western Christians, there seems to be a feeling that, if they don't have all the answers, they shouldn't speak. Many people feel that they can't fully commit to Christianity because they don't understand all of the doctrines or they find some inconsistency in their understanding. They fear being mocked, or looking stupid, and dwell in a place of doubt. The praise that we offer comes from a moment of certainty though, a personal experience that we can testify to. If we have experienced God's amazing grace, then we can proclaim with confidence what he has done for us. One thing we do know. We were blind, but now we see. Nothing else matters.

1. Do you ever feel embarrassed for not having "all the answers?"
2. Has there been a time you can point to that you've experienced God's amazing grace in your life?

## Natural Worship

Read: John 9:35-41

Focus: John 9:38

*Then the man said, "Lord, I believe," and he worshiped him.*

It was all darkness and light. The man who had been healed had light in his eyes for the first time in his life, and the world was open before him. At the same time, the assembly of God had been closed behind him when the religious leaders threw him out. In this time of in-between, Jesus came and found him. Jesus posed a roundabout question to him: "Do you believe in the Son of Man?" The man's response was profound. It showed that he was both seeking something to believe in, and willing to follow Jesus to whatever that was. When Jesus announced himself as the Son of Man, whom Daniel had seen seated on the throne, the man did what the Pharisees refused to do. He believed.

The telling thing about his belief is that it motivated him to do something. It wasn't a grand mission of witnessing or an action of self-sacrifice; it was the outpouring of a grateful heart. The man worshipped Jesus. Because he believed that Jesus was the messiah, he couldn't help but give him the glory he is due. Worship is the appropriate and natural expression of our belief that God is worthy. If we truly believe God is who he says he is, and has done the things he says he has, and has loved us personally the way he says he does, then our hearts worship. Take time to think about Jesus and what he's done for you: all that he sacrificed, the depth of his love, the healing he offers. How will you respond?

1. Why do you worship God?
2. Think back to the moment that you first believed. What feeling was in your heart in that instant?

**Full Worship**

Read: John 10:1-10

Focus: John 10:10

*[Jesus said,]The thief comes only to steal and kill and destroy; I have come that they may have life, and have it to the full.*

Jesus takes the Pharisees to task for trying to hem themselves in with the safety of The Rules. He claims that the life he came to give is more "full" than the one they teach about; that, in removing their safety net, he offers something better. There is a temptation, when we hear about having life to the full, to think of a life full of only good things or a life full of happiness without pain. Jesus lived life to the full. He didn't hold back or shy away from extremes. He experienced amazing joy and incredible sadness. He gained friends and lost them. He was praised and shunned. Somehow, through it all, he gave thanks to God, and in him we have our example.

Just as having a full life means experiencing the full range of emotion and experience, offering God full worship in song means expressing the full range of experience in musicality. It means praising God for all the good that he's given us. It means blessing God in God's fullness: Father, Son, and Holy Spirit. It means singing of all he's done, is doing, and is yet to do. It means acknowledging pain and offering it to God for healing. It means loud and soft and fast and slow and old and new and everything in between. Music is a gift of God that gives us a chance to acknowledge and give voice to all of the fullness of life and honour God in it. How amazing!

1. Is it appropriate to sing about pain in church? How much?
2. Are you able to worship in the midst of grief and tragedy? How?

**All In**

Read: John 10:11-21

Focus: John 10:13

*The man runs away because he is a hired hand and cares nothing for the sheep.*

In this passage, Jesus highlights the differences between the ones who are vying for the hearts of God's people: himself and the Pharisees. To Jesus, one of the key issues was that of commitment, which he talked about using a comparison of the shepherd to the hired hand. Both of these had care over a group of sheep, but one took care of the sheep out of love and long term interest, and the other out of self-interest. The shepherd is willing to go to the mat for the sheep; he's all in. The hired man is only interested in the sheep as far as they further *his* goals. He'll do the job for the paycheck, or out of obligation, but when hard times come he's going to look out for number one.

Within church ministry, we can follow either of these examples. We can be Christ-like servants, or people filling the job because we like what we're getting out of it. This doesn't necessarily mean money. Some people serve because it's fun. Others serve because they like the accolades or the way people look up to them. Still others volunteer because they feel like God expects it of them, and they have to. Elements of these aren't bad in and of themselves, but God isn't looking for servants with that primary motivation. God wants people who are in it for love of him and his people, not love of themselves. It's then that they will do everything that they can to nurture growth. We are at our best in service when self falls away and we are seeking our people's best.

1. Why do you serve your church?
2. What do you think it looks like when someone is serving as a "hired hand?"

**An Unexpected Voice**

Read: John 10:22-42

Focus: John 10:25-27

*Jesus answered, "I did tell you, but you do not believe. The works I do in my Father's name testify about me, but you do not believe because you are not my sheep. My sheep listen to my voice; I know them, and they follow me.*

Around Hanukkah, Jesus was spending time in the Temple. It was a time of re-dedication: a celebration of God's provision and his deliverance. With minds looking back to the origins of the festival, the Jews approached Jesus and asked him to declare himself, hoping for liberation from their Roman oppressors. They asked Jesus to "tell them plainly," as if he hadn't been saying it for the past year. He had, but not in a way they wanted to hear. There were words they were waiting for, signs they were eagerly expecting, but those words and signs weren't coming. Instead Jesus was spouting the kind of deceptive heresy that got Israel in trouble. How could he be the messiah?

We all have expectations of God: the way he works, the way he speaks, what he wants from us and more. We look for signs of God at work in our services, and can easily grow discouraged if people aren't seeming emotionally moved or pouring forward to the altar. We dissect scripture, looking for firm answers to things that God has left ambiguous, not willing to leave faith in tension. If we're not "feeling" God or getting the answers we're looking for, we can feel abandoned. If we perceive our congregation to be in that situation, we can feel like failures. God is always speaking, though. Transformation comes when we can put aside our expectations of what that he should sound like, and just listen for his voice. God knows us, and his plans are so much greater than our expectations.

1. What are some things that you expect from God?
2. When have you seen God move in an unexpected way?

## Expectation

Read: John 11:1-44

Focus: John 11:40

*Then Jesus said, "Did I not tell you that if you believe, you will see the glory of God?"*

Some people come to church to be instructed. Some people come to experience fellowship. Some people come for the music. Many people come expecting to experience the glory of God in a way that they don't in their day-to-day lives. The glory of God is all around us. Scripture has a lot to say on the subject. David tells us that the heavens declare it. Paul tells us that we fall short of it, and everything that we do should be for it. John tells us that our future home will shine with it. Why, then, would we expect to experience it more at a Sunday service than on the drive home, and how do we deal with it when we're not even experiencing it there?

It could be as simple as our mindset. Is it just a matter of believing that the glory of God is here now, waiting on our belief to be manifest? The truth is that Sunday services **can** be a unique opportunity to experience the glory of God, simply because a group of his children are gathered with the intention of joining together to seek it. There is a very different feel to worship when we enter in with an air of expectation than when we offer it by rote, or even with simple hope. If we want to see the glory of God in our church, we need to be praying for the sight to see it, believing it's there. We can praise him with certain knowledge that God's Spirit is moving among us, and we will experience his glory.

1. What gets in the way of believing?
2. How do we deal with the time that we do believe but it seems like we're not "seeing the Glory of God?"

**Worthier**

Read: John 12:1-11

Focus: John 12:3

*Then Mary took about a pint of pure nard, an expensive perfume; she poured it on Jesus' feet and wiped his feet with her hair. And the house was filled with the fragrance of the perfume.*

At its very core, worship is relative. Humans naturally think of worth comparatively, whether in monetary terms (this object or experience is worth more or less than $20), or in terms of personal cost (this act is worth more or less of my time and effort). Mary's outpouring was an act of extravagant worship. What Mary was saying by sacrificing this expensive perfume to no apparent purpose was simply that Jesus was worth much more to her than the cost of the fragrance. In wiping his feet with her hair, she showed that his honor was worth more than her dignity. Judas' thought was of what else could have been done with that value, things that were worth more to him than honouring Jesus.

Each person in each church has an expectation of what is appropriate in worship. Each person has a comfort zone of what they are willing to express and what they're comfortable with the people around them expressing. Moving out of that comfort zone is difficult, but it is at the centre of the worship experience. It's about leaving ourselves behind: becoming less as he becomes more. Stretching and growing in our worship to God shows his worth to us. Sometimes worshipping God isn't about being practical. An act of worship requires sacrifice. That's what shows which thing is worthier. It might be money or time or talent or goods or dignity, but the heart of it is saying to God, "You are worth more to me than this."

1. What are some ways that you have stretched your comfort zone in worship?
2. What are some things that are hard to give up to God in worship?

**The Expected Savior**

Read: John 12:12-19

Focus: John 12:16

*At first his disciples did not understand all this. Only after Jesus was glorified did they realize that these things had been written about him and that these things had been done to him.*

As Jesus entered Jerusalem, he was greeted with shouts of "hosanna," and a flood of expectation. It was a cry of longing for a savior, and an expression of hope and belief that the savior had come. Unfortunately, no one really understood what that meant. Everyone in the crowd had a different expectation of what they needed to be saved from and the method their savior would use to do it. Strangers who had only heard rumours of what he had done hailed him as the one who would drive out the Romans and free the nation. His followers only seemed to expect greater majesty. Jesus confounded their expectations. Rather than coming as a conqueror, he came as a sacrifice - clothed in humility rather than crowned, on a donkey rather than in a chariot.

The people had taken their preconceived notions of what the messiah should be, and draped them around Jesus. They saw what they wanted to see. Even those who should have known better did it. And often so do we. Rather than coming to him to be taught and taking him at his word, we apply *our* ideas of who God *should* be, and base our expectations there. We get confused and angry when God doesn't live up to our assumptions. In the midst of those times, we need to remember his passion: that the fullness of his promise may not be what we'd choose for ourselves, and that his greatness is more than we can imagine.

1. Have you ever had a time that you've been disappointed with God?
2. Can you think of a time when you've seen God work in an unexpected way?

### He Glorifies

Read: John 12:20-36

Focus: John 12:28

*[Jesus said,] "Father, glorify your name!" Then a voice came from heaven, "I have glorified it, and will glorify it again."*

As worshippers – as the people of God – our primary purpose is to glorify God. We pray and sing songs to express his great place in our hearts. We try to live and serve in ways that show people how incredible he is. We exist in the world as monuments to his transforming power. That can be a lot of pressure. Sometimes we can feel like the world is watching us to catch us messing up, or that our talents and abilities don't do justice to his glory. In a nutshell, we can feel inadequate to the task.

In this passage, Jesus highlights a key truth about worship: God is and always has been fully capable of glorifying himself. The greatest thing that we can do for God's glory is to allow him to work in us and show it to the world. God's name is glorified when we offer ourselves to him to use for that purpose. Jesus' prayer is a model of self sacrifice. He doesn't say that it's too hard, or too much, or that he is incapable of doing what needs to be done. As worship leaders, there are going to be Sundays that we just don't feel up to it. There are going to be weeks when, if it's all up to us, it's just not going to be good enough. The great news is that in times when we face opposition, or physical, emotional or financial limitations, we can call "Father, glorify your name!" and God answers in a voice like thunder.

1. How has God glorified himself through your life?
2. What are some of the keys you've found in your ministry to opening yourself up to be used by God?

**Where The Heart Is**

Read: John 12:37-50

Focus: John 12:43

*...for they loved human praise more than praise from God.*

As the people experienced the ministry and miracles of Jesus, some still rejected him. Many, though, when they came face to face with the reality of who he is, couldn't help but believe. Once they had come to believe, they faced a decision about what was going to be most important in their lives. This choice was particularly difficult for those with established places in the Jewish leadership. Believing in Jesus would mean losing the backing of the most powerful Hebrew religious faction of the time. It would mean losing their positions of honour and their standing in the community. They had to choose between devoting themselves to being admired by people or devoting themselves to God, regardless of the expense.

Motivations are important. Each time we take the platform or the pulpit, we put ourselves before the eyes of the people and know we'll be judged. For many with artistic temperaments, being praised for a great worship service is a high. Truthfully, most people run on approval to some extent or another. As we're processing the feedback, we need to do a gut check to see whose praise is more important to us: human praise, or praise from God. Worship is a tricky thing: we can sing the same words and play the same notes, but if our heart is focused on people, we're worshipping them, not God. We can make an idol of their praise. If this is the case, it can have a huge impact on the heart of worship our congregation has. The ultimate result is that we either lead them back to themselves, or we lead them towards God.

1. What are some ways that you can tell where your heart is in worship?
2. How can we work to put our heart's focus where it belongs?

**Washed Clean**

Read: John 13:1-17

Focus: John 13:10

*Jesus answered, "Those who have had a bath need only to wash their feet; their whole body is clean. And you are clean …*

As Jesus enters into his final hours with his friends before his betrayal, he takes the time to give one more object lesson. He gets a basin of water and a towel and, in an act of love, begins to wash the dust and dirt from their feet. Peter, being Peter, is alternately appalled and overzealous. He quickly moves from the idea that he's unworthy to be washed by Jesus, to the desire for a washing of his whole body. Jesus tells Peter that he doesn't need that kind of washing. Peter is clean; it's only the dust of the day that he needs removed.

As Jesus' disciples, we are already washed clean. When we come into his house, we don't need to come in ashamed and feeling filthy. His blood has already taken away the filth of our guilt. At the same time, though, coming into the house of God requires another examination. When we sit at his table, he still desires to take care of the dust of the day. We are clean, but our feet may be dirty. It can be a difficult thing to hold that in tension; confident in our salvation, but aware of our need. As we come to worship, he is waiting to wash our sins anew; we come, not as beggars, but as friends. We come with the burdens of our week, the sins and failings of broken people being made new by the God who gives us this example of servant love. We come to the healing water of Christ.

1. Does the idea of Jesus serving you make you uncomfortable?
2. What effect does this example of service have on how we approach worship?

## Through God's Eyes

Read: John 13:18-30

Focus: John 13:18

*[Jesus said,] "I am not referring to all of you; I know those I have chosen. But this is to fulfill this passage of Scripture: 'He who shared my bread has turned against me."*

The disciples hadn't come to the meal knowing that it was the last time that they'd sit around the table with Jesus. Each of them came with their own beliefs, understandings, and agendas, and Jesus served them all. Judas must have been extremely conflicted, sitting there among his companions, having had his feet washed by the rabbi he'd been following and sharing in the meal that told of the deliverance of his people. He knew that his heart was not in accord with theirs. Jesus had no such conflict. He knew the heart of Judas and still welcomed him at his table. We remember this meal in our congregations as "Communion," a time to draw together with God and with believers around the world.

All of worship is communion, though. Through song, word, and sacrament, we come together before God to give praise and receive sustenance. Sometimes we'll look around the room and see people whose faces don't reflect that. Sometimes we'll look around and see people who outwardly seem to be joining in, but we know are separated from Christ. Sometimes we'll come knowing that we ourselves have not been fully in communion with him. All of that being so, we remember that we are worshiping a God who invites everyone to his table. As facilitators of worship, we welcome all into his presence, including, and especially, ourselves. If we can begin to look at all God's people with God's eyes, two things happen: our communion with each other draws closer through him, and our praise for him grows deeper in appreciation of his grace.

1. Have you ever felt unworthy to be on a worship team?
2. Does it ever bother you to see "certain people" in a worship service? How do you deal with those feelings?

**Love Reign In Us**

Read: John 13:31-35

Focus: John 13:34

*[Jesus said,] "A new command I give you: Love one another. As I have loved you, so you must love one another."*

With the departure of Judas, Jesus had one last opportunity to discuss his legacy with his true followers. He warned them that the time had come for him to leave them, and gave them one final command: that they love each other with a Godly love – the kind of love that Paul would talk about in 1st Corinthians 13. Jesus says that it was this special love that his followers would be known by. It would be the qualifier that showed who his real disciples were. It was non-optional. It was probably the most difficult command that he ever gave.

In a perfect world, worship teams would blend seamlessly in terms of vision, stylistic approach to worship, and instrumental and vocal harmony. Everyone would work together well and enjoy each other's company. In the world we live in, sometimes that doesn't happen. Guitar players and piano players will have different opinions of who gets to drive the song. Drummers will have different ideas of how the song should feel. Singers will have learned a different version. Bass players will smell funny. How we deal with these conflicts, and how we deal with the people involved in the conflicts, spills out into our public worship ministry. Conflict distracts us from worship. In practical terms, it can affect how we play and sing, but it also can stop us from being able to focus on God. When we have focus problems, the congregation picks up on that. Even when it's difficult, God's love must reign in us for us to serve his people best.

1. How should disagreements about style or arrangement be dealt with?
2. Have you ever been on a team where two members didn't get along? How was it handled?

## Great Expectations

Read: John 13:36-38;18:15-18,25-27;21:15-19

Focus: John 13:38

*Jesus answered, 'Will you really lay down your life for me? Very truly I tell you, before the rooster crows, you will disown me three times!*

Peter had a tendency to let his mouth run in front of him. When he proclaimed his allegiance, he meant it. When he said he'd go with Jesus to death, he believed he was speaking the truth. He had every intention of following through on what he said. Life just didn't play out the way he thought it would. Peter didn't know himself as well as he thought he did. When the test came, Peter failed. Jesus knew he would, and he called Peter anyway. Even after the failure, Simon Peter was the one that Jesus asked to feed his sheep.

Within the Christian community, we tend to put our leaders on pedestals. We have great expectations of them, and when we're in leadership we tend to place expectations on ourselves. Unfortunately, often we fail to meet those standards. Sometimes it's in small things, sometime large. Sometimes those failures are private, and sometimes they are very, very public. Despite our best intentions, we will mess up. Jesus knew we would, and he called us anyway. The important thing is not to let that infirmity become a way of life. We worship a God that forgives and restores. We serve a God who sees the best of our potential and calls us to it. If we fall, we need to call on him for help. If we have been lifted by God "out of the mud and mire," how much louder must we praise him!

1. What does the reaction of the people tend to be when a Christian "celebrity" fails?
2. How should churches deal with worship team members that fail to live up to their proclamation?

## Do Not Let

Read: John 14:1-14

Focus: John 14:1

*[Jesus said,] "Do not let your hearts be troubled. You believe in God; believe also in me."*

Jesus' disciples were growing worried. The rug was about to be pulled out from underneath them. They'd given up their careers and left their families to follow Jesus, and now he was telling them that he was leaving. In the face of this, he offered this comfort: whether he's there in person or not doesn't matter. What he's doing is through the power of the Father, and the Father isn't going anywhere. Not only that, but in the same way that he acts on behalf of the Father, he is giving them the authority to act on his behalf. The goal is the same, the Glory of the Father.

As worship teams, we have a special calling along those same lines. We've been commissioned to use the gifts that God has given us to bring glory to the Father through the Son. When it comes time to step out in front of the congregation, though, sometimes it can feel like we don't have it in us to do it the way he's asked. Our hearts are troubled. The worries of the world and pressures of life distract and hinder our worship. Jesus uses an odd phrase, though: "Do not let..." He implies that it's a choice. Whatever issue we are facing, we can decide whether to let it weigh on us or give it over to God. On Sunday, for an hour or two, choose not to let your hearts be troubled. We can leave our burdens at the foot of the cross. If we want them later, we can most likely choose to go get them again.

1. Is there anything troubling your heart today?
2. What does it mean to you to believe in God?

## Reconnect

Read: John 14:15-31

Focus: John 14:18

*[Jesus said,] "I will not leave you as orphans; I will come to you."*

For the children of God on Sunday mornings, coming to church is like coming home. They enter into their Father's house on earth and they'll feel things that they might feel walking into their own parents houses. Those of them who are in good, close relationships with God will feel welcome and peace and a sense of drawing near. For some though, walking into church may be a reminder that their relationship is tense, or broken, or absent altogether. For the first group, engaging in worship is easy. For the second, it can be difficult: a chore, or an empty exercise. It is hard for them to give praise to a God that they feel has gone away and left them to face life alone.

One of the joys of worship is that it can be a time of reconnection. We can come to declare the greatness and faithfulness of God, knowing that he keeps his promises, and one of his promises is that he will not leave us as orphans. We are family, and he wants to connect with us. It's important to remember that that reconnection isn't usually instant, though. Most of the time, we don't go from zero to passionate worship in 2.5 verses. We need to give our people, and ourselves, room to journey in it. Worship is a function of relationship; an outpouring of the alignment of our hearts. James 4:8 tells us that as we draw near to God, he will draw near to us. As we open ourselves to the truth and beauty of this love relationship, our praise becomes free, whole, and an overwhelming presence in our lives. He will come.

1. What helps you draw near to God when you feel far away?
2. What can we do to help our people nurture this relationship in worship?

**Remain**

Read: John 15:1-17

Focus: John 15:5

*[Jesus said,] "I am the vine; you are the branches. If you remain in me and I in you, you will bear much fruit; apart from me you can do nothing."*

Being on a worship team committed to excellence can be hard work. It can also be dangerous. Relying on ourselves is easy. It gives us control. If we work hard enough, it can even yield some outwardly impressive results. In this reading, Jesus challenges that. Sometimes, with our talent, skill development, rehearsal and production, it's hard to remember that God does the real work. Giving our best is honouring to God and an act of worship we're called to, but it's not what produces the real fruit in our ministry. In a role where we help to connect people's hearts to God's heart, our hearts are even more important than our hands and voices.

Jesus says that the key to bearing fruit is remaining in him. That means more than a point of connection here and a prayer there. It means a lifestyle of relationship with him. As worship team members, our daily walk with God forms the basis of our music - our reason to sing. When we lead people in worship, it should be from the overflow of our hearts. To be at our most effective, at least as much effort as goes in to practicing and rehearsing needs to go into our devotional time and personal faith development. In the midst of our worry over arrangement and flow, we can take comfort in this promise: whatever else happens musically, if we remain in him, he will have his hand on the result. He will guide us in our preparation, he will carry us through our execution and he will amplify our production.

1. What do you do to maintain your relationship with God?
2. What kind of "fruit" do you think a worship ministry should see?

## Worship Testifies

Read: John 15:18-16:4

Focus: John 15:27

*[Jesus said,] "And you also must testify, for you have been with me from the beginning."*

Music tends to connect us with our experiences. Certain lyrics ring out with power because they speak to the ways we've seen or are seeing God move in our lives. Certain songs bring us back to a time that we experienced God in a new or deeper way. Beyond that, our worship is an opportunity to experience joining with God and his purposes. Jesus bore witness to who the Father is and his will for his people. The Holy Spirit bears witness to the truth of who Jesus is. In turn, we bear witness to everyone that God's truth and power are real in our lives. The songs we sing together serve to tell the world our God story.

There is something profound that happens when the body of Christ responds to him in authentic worship; when God's people gather together and, with one voice, praise him for who he is, and all he's done and is yet to do. Their declaration is a testimony to the world of a God who is worthy of praise. Not only that, but when we join with the Holy Spirit in witness of his greatness, he moves. Many people who have entered into a real relationship with God have been moved to that decision in a time of corporate worship, where the witness of the Holy Spirit and the witness of the body have led them to open themselves to God in a new way. We sing praise, and our worship says something to the world. They may not like it. They may even mock it, but for some it will be the most compelling argument that they will know until they experience it for themselves.

1. What is one time that you've witnessed God at work?
2. What is one worship song that you connect to in a special way because of your experience?

## Head/Heart Divide

Read: John 16:5-16

Focus: John 16:13a

*But when he, the Spirit of truth, comes, he will guide you into all the truth.*

On this night with Jesus, his disciples stood at a head/heart threshold. They had knowledge of Jesus. They'd followed him. They'd learned from him. They acknowledged him as Christ, but they didn't understand him. They didn't understand his mission. Jesus was taking this last opportunity to prod them past the point of following him to joining him. He had a warning and a promise; the world and the Spirit. For his followers, it wasn't enough to know about Jesus after he had gone: there was still so much more for God to show them!

Times of worship can sometimes be seen as a lesser part of church. Some people hold them as an obligation to tradition. Some look at them as performances to be enjoyed. For some people, the time of worship in song is more of a volley to set up the pastor's sermon spike. All of those things may have elements of truth, but at the heart of it, congregational worship is a vital time with God in its own right. Worship is should be an experience with the Spirit of God. It's good to come and learn about God, but opening up and worshipping in song provides an opportunity for God to interact with our hearts. When we connect with the Holy Spirit through worship, he can use that time to illuminate our hearts, teach us in an intimate way that goes beyond words, and connect our spirits with his truth. It's a time when he can speak privately, in different ways, on different subjects, to every believer in the room: a time that the relationship of the heart overcomes the knowledge of the head.

1. Have you ever had an encounter with the Spirit of God during worship? What was it like?
2. What is one thing that God has shown you during a time of worship?

## Living In The Promise

Read: John 16:17-33

Focus: John 16:33

*[Jesus said,] "I have told you these things, so that in me you may have peace. In this world you will have trouble. But take heart! I have overcome the world."*

It must have been hard for the disciples to hear all this. Jesus had become the center of their lives. Their faith was placed in him; not as a future hope, but a present rock. Their tomorrows revolved around him, and he was telling them that he wouldn't be there. This marked an important shift for the followers of Jesus, from being people who's attention was on today to ones whose attention was focused forward. They were about to enter a time of trouble. There would be intense persecution and their world would feel like it was falling apart. "Take heart," Jesus says, though. Even though what is coming is bad, what is coming after that is the more important thing.

Many times, when the people of God come to a time of worship, it's in the in-between. We come to praise God in times of trouble, doubt, and storm. In the midst of that, people may not feel like praising, but who God is doesn't change. His presence and promises are just as valid in the time of waiting as the minute of fruition. As we lead our congregations in worship, remember that we can speak from a place of process with certainty of the end. We don't have to pretend that there is no trouble in the world, but we can use the time of worship to proclaim the victory that Christ has given us while we wait to see it in our lives. As we proclaim his promises, it gives people an opportunity to claim them, and reminds them of the truth of the hope they have in Christ.

1. Is it ever hard for you to hold on to God's promises?
2. Can you think of a "claiming the promise" song that's been meaningful to you?

**That They Would Be One**

Read: John 17:1-26

Focus: John 17:20-21

*[Jesus said,] "My prayer is not for them alone. I pray also for those who will believe in me through their message, that all of them may be one, Father, just as you are in me and I am in you. May they also be in us so that the world may believe that you have sent me."*

As Jesus closed his final meal with his disciples, he prayed a prayer spanning himself, his disciples, and all of those who would be impacted by their lives and ministries. He brought them from a place of thinking about themselves and how his departure was going to impact them to prompting them to consider their role in the bigger picture of God's plan for redemption. They were going to model and prove God's love for the world, just as he had, and those that came after would follow their pattern. The heart of Jesus' prayer was that they would be bound in unity by their love, and that bond would be the evidence of his truth.

Unfortunately, when the world looks at Christianity, they see splits in both large denominations and small churches. We are far from being known for our unity. Many churches have been ravaged by "worship wars," or at least had a low-grade "police action" in the background for some time. Worship wars aren't usually about doctrinal issues, but preference issues. Neither side is willing to back down or compromise to suit the other. There is a break in unity because there is a break in love. However, when we truly love someone, we desire their best and not our own. For those in leadership, it's up to us to set that tone. Maybe that means that we don't feel like we get to fully sink into our "natural" mode of worship, but in honouring Christ's prayer for unity in love, we engage in a deeper, truer form of worship.

1. Do you ever feel like you don't get to express yourself in the style you'd like to?
2. How do you feel about playing songs you don't personally find appealing?

## Where God Is

Read: John 18:1-14

Focus: John 18:1-2

*When he had finished praying, Jesus left with his disciples and crossed the Kidron Valley. On the other side there was a garden, and he and his disciples went into it … Jesus had often met there with his disciples.*

Jesus and his disciples had a garden that they would meet. For them, it was worth the journey across the Kidron Valley to spend time together there. Maybe it was a place of peace, or beauty, or shade, or a place where the fruitfulness of the land brought about thoughts of the creative power of God. It was a place of connection for them. In a similar way, there are times that the environment around us speaks powerfully of God and his nature, and helps us welcome the moving of his Spirit. For some, it's found on a mountaintop, others by a river. For some, the vaulted ceilings of an old cathedral speak to God's majesty, for others it's flashing lights and fog machines. For many, coming back to a location where they have had an encounter with God brings back the feeling of closeness that they had then.

In a way, each week Jesus takes us on a journey to the same place again. We come into our church building to meet with him in a special way, joining together to praise him and come to know him more. As we approach worship, often a lot of thought can go in to how we sound and what we say, and less into what the environment of our church communicates about God and how it encourages people to relate to him. We need to be conscious of how our environment affects the way people approach God. How a church looks and feels - the dress, decor and layout - can be as much a barrier or facilitator of worship as the music we offer.

1. Is there a specific location that you go to experience God's presence?
2. Within a worship service, what elements of environment help people to connect with the presence of God?

**Unto The King**

Read: John 18:28-40

Focus: John 18:37

*"You are a king, then!" said Pilate. Jesus answered, "You say that I am a king. In fact, the reason I was born and came into the world is to testify to the truth. Everyone on the side of truth listens to me."*

The Romans had very little interest in the inner workings of the Hebrew religion. In order to get them to intervene, the Jewish leaders had to bring a civil charge against Jesus. They offered him up as one who was in political rebellion against the authority of Rome: that he styled himself "The King of the Jews." It was an interesting accusation, because at the same time it was completely deceptive and profoundly true. He didn't claim any civil authority over the nation of Israel, but who he was spiritually went far beyond being a simple teacher.

In contemporary worship, there is a tendency to focus on the friendship of Christ, or the teaching of Christ, or the sacrifice of Christ. Our culture likes that and connects well with it. It puts the love of Jesus at the front of our vision of him, and that has value. In the midst of it, though, we can lose the view of Jesus as king. There's a big difference between how we worship "Jesus our best friend and redeemer," and "Jesus the King of Creation and Lord of our lives." Worshipping Jesus as King requires a change in mindset. It means recognizing his authority in our lives and churches. It means acknowledging his position and power. It means admitting that he is more and we are less, on a scale that we can hardly imagine. It's a difficult tension to hold: the king that becomes a friend, rather than the friend that happens to be a king, but when we take hold of that truth it makes his love and sacrifice that much more amazing.

1. How would you interact with royalty?
2. What are some ways that our worship service can reflect the majesty of God?

## Taking Care

Read: John 19:1-37

Focus: John 19:26-27

*When Jesus saw his mother there, and the disciple whom he loved standing nearby, he said to her, "Woman, here is your son," and to the disciple, "Here is your mother." From that time on, this disciple took her into his home.*

As a person reads through the Gospels and looks at Jesus' life, one thing becomes abundantly clear: Jesus cared about people. His every action showed how much he valued the people around him, particularly those whose lives were especially intertwined with his own. Jesus looked down from the cross and saw his mother and one of his best friends. As the oldest son, it had fallen to him to be sure she was cared for in her old age, and he couldn't do it himself. In John, he saw a man that he had taught how to love, and now he entrusted to John the love and care of the one who had cared for him since birth.

John responded to this commission wholeheartedly, and made Mary part of his family. He could have discharged his duty by arranging for a stipend for her, or overseen her care being passed to the believers as a group, or taking up a collection, but he honored Jesus by taking her into his own home. His love dictated his actions. How we deal with what Jesus has charged us with, big or small, reveals a lot about our relationship with him. If he has called us to minister to his body by leading them in worship, there's a lot of ways to go about it that seem "good enough," but as we prepare, we need to consider what is good enough for the one who gave everything. Love for him needs to guide the way we take care of what he's given us.

1. Are there ever ways that we skimp on the effort we could give God as a praise team?
2. How do you think God responds when we give him all that we can?

**Beyond A Doubt**

Read: John 20:1-31

Focus: John 20:25,27-28

*But he said to them, "Unless I see the nail marks in his hands and put my finger where the nails were, and put my hand into his side, I will not believe." . . . Then [Jesus] said to Thomas, "Put your finger here; see my hands. Reach out your hand and put it into my side. Stop doubting and believe." Thomas said to him, "My Lord and my God!"*

Thomas gets a bad rap in a popular Christian culture as the guy who wouldn't believe when the other apostles told him that Jesus had risen from the dead. Despite having walked with Jesus and seen all that he had done, from healing the sick to raising the dead, Thomas just couldn't get his head around Jesus' resurrection. Really, it was understandable. There is a long history of dead people staying dead. Thomas has one big thing going for him, though: he laid out the criteria for his belief, and when it was met he didn't move the goalposts; he proclaimed Jesus as God.

We all can have a tendency to doubt, usually matched only by a desire to see God work. The problem is that our doubt is so practiced, we often have trouble recognising God when we see him. We hear stories about the work of the Holy Spirit in other places, and can be tempted to chalk it up to anything from emotional manipulation to mass hysteria. It's in our nature to seek rational explanations for everything. Unfortunately, when we live in that headspace it becomes almost impossible for God to show himself to us, even in our own worship. We doubt our experiences, then complain that God is distant. What will it take for us to look up in worship and say to him, "My Lord and my God!"?

1. How can you tell if God is moving in worship?
2. Do you ever have trouble discerning when God is working?

## This And More

Read: John 21:1-14, 20-25

Focus: John 21:25

*Jesus did many other things as well. If every one of them were written down, I suppose that even the whole world would not have room for the books that would be written.*

John finishes off his gospel account with an important note: this wasn't all! The things that John had written were a sampling; a survey of the ministry of Jesus Christ that didn't come close to encompassing all that Jesus had done. John suggests that there isn't enough writing surface in the world to record the fullness of Christ's ministry. Miracles, times of teaching, and everyday interactions must have gone unrecorded. The picture we are left with of Jesus is sufficient to know him, but if we imagine that we know the totality of who he is and what he is able to do, we are sorely mistaken.

In many churches, the size of our Jesus is small. Our view of him is limited by our understanding. We give our lives to the Jesus we know, then we seek to box him in and so control the impact that he has on them. When this happens, how we worship changes. The words we use change, because they start to feel adequate. Our plans and how we approach worship become smaller and more contained. Our expectations of worship shrink. The God we worship, though, is the same God that John can barely sum up in earthly presence. He is the same God that Paul says in Ephesians 3:20 can do infinitely more than we can ask or imagine. So let us approach God with awe, knowing that however much we love him, he loves more. Whatever we see him as capable of, he can do more. Whoever we think he is, he is more.

1. In what ways might we limit God in our worship?
2. What aspects of our worship begin to hint at the majesty of God?

## Worshipping Through John

John 13:1

*Having loved his own who were in the world, he loved them to the end.*

Over the course of this devotional, we've had a chance to look at the life of Jesus Christ through John's eyes and talk about how his life and teachings relate to the modern worship experience. One thing that has stood out during the process is the role that love plays in worship. True worship comes from love, and we can only truly love what we know. One of the greatest things that Jesus did is open the way for our love by making the Father known. As we carry on, may our worship resonate with the cycle of outpoured love that flows from the Father, through the Son and the Spirit, and back from grateful hearts.

1. Over the course of this devotional series, has the way you approach or view worship changed?
2. How does the way you view God change the way you approach worship?
3. What are some ways that Jesus modeled worship?
4. What are some reasons John has offered that we should worship Jesus?

Made in the USA
Monee, IL
12 December 2019